T0374194

SHELTER

CHARLOTTE ANN

authorHOUSE®

AuthorHouse™
1663 Liberty Drive
Bloomington, IN 47403
www.authorhouse.com
Phone: 1 (800) 839-8640

Published by AuthorHouse 03/23/2020

ISBN: 978-1-5462-3778-5 (sc)
ISBN: 978-1-5462-3777-8 (e)

Print information available on the last page.

Contents

Acknowledgements

First of all, I must thank Candace Baker Bradley, for believing in me before I believed in myself. You always had my back, my little sister of the heart. You were my mama, my forever friend, from toddlers to teens and back to old lady toddlers! I thank my sisters, Ann, Jean, dearly departed Linda, Julie and my brother, Roger. Thank you for never letting go and I love you all so much. I thank my sister of the soul, Kelly Clayton, and her sweet family. Oh the stories we could tell ...or maybe not! I thank my first editor, Angelia Phillips of Pumpkin Run Pulse. Thank you for putting up with me and helping me write right! You always knew how to slice and dice without cutting the spirit out of my writing. I must thank my editors from Author House. I only sat on this book for years and you helped me get up and just Do it!

Last but certainly not least, I must thank each and every one who has ever assisted and helped an orphaned child or pet. How many homeless animals and children would have gone uncared for, except for you? Because of you, they had shelter, food and learned how to love, by being loved by you. You are God's very hands and I know He puts a calling on your hearts, enabling you to help unwanted animals and children. You are their voice. I thank you a million times, to the moon and mars and back again, Amen.

Introduction

I was one of the luckier orphans. My first and only foster mother met me as an infant and kept me forever. I was told, my biological parents met each other while they were staying at an orphanage called Saint Joseph's Villa, here in Richmond, Virginia. My father's parents were deceased, and at that time, his brothers and sisters were unable to care for him. My mother was orphaned and adopted by a man in Staunton, Virginia. But for some reason, wound up in Saint Joseph's, orphaned again. My parents fell in love and married there, with their orphan friends and guardians cheering them on. My father's name was Joseph and my mother's name was Dorothy. He was 20 years old, and she was 17, when I was born in June of 1950.

My last contact with my mother, was when I was six years old and starting first grade. She came to visit me at my foster home, after not contacting me for several months. Feeling angry at her infrequent visits and disinterest in me, I refused to talk or even look at her. I did manage to tell her, she "bothered me." I never saw or heard from her again. She disappeared as if she was never there.

I last heard from my father when I was eight years old. He had a serious drinking problem and seldom visited me. He called me one evening while he seemingly was very drunk. I could hardly understand him, his voice was so garbled, I unfortunately, hung up on him. I never heard from him again.

So they were the first denial of my heart, "they did not matter." "I had a whole family", and I did. "My family loved me," and they did! I had four older sisters and a younger brother, who needed anyone else? It took me thirty odd years to be brave enough to face the pain of being abandoned. I never forgot my biological parents, but I did not know pain was there, fragmenting my heart. I believe I carried the "great guilt," "I was bad, so they never came back to get me."

I started writing at 12 years old. These are poems, prose and some of my 2016 blog posts and thoughts of lessons learned, feelings felt, experiences lived. I believe both of my biological parents are deceased now. It is not my intent to blame them or anyone else for our loss of each other. However, I do regret our loss.

I have often asked Jesus, what was His intent for me to experience such heartache? If you see yourself in any of my writing, I pray it comforts, maybe enlightens and even makes you smile and laugh.

May Jesus bless you as He has blessed me; by cleaning out your heart and refilling it with His magnificent love, turning your weakness into great strength, to give away.

God Bless,
Charlotte Ann

If You're All Alone

{Dedicated to Lena Marie Clayton]

If you're all alone,
if you're little or grown,
or just hide a small child in your heart.

If you secretly feel
perhaps you're not real,
and your insides just fall all apart.

If you aren't good enough
so you play like you're tough,
while you often daydream you're the best.

You're too fat, you're too thin
you're too lazy to begin,
and so dumb you would fail your own test!

Then spend time with me
come in and let's see,
if we can find something to love.

Let's laugh and let's cry,
we'll turn cartwheels and fly
and cherish our Father above.

Four

My earliest memory of my life was at the age of four. I was helping clean house, picking up toys and trash, thinking to myself, "I've always been four." I couldn't remember ever being anything else. What does "always" mean to a four year old? When we grow up, we forget things we knew then.

It was around that time, my foster mother informed me that my biological mother had called, complaining to her. I was behaving badly and talking to her very smart-aleck when we would go out together. I offered no explanation to my foster mother. Nor did she press me for any. She knew and understood all too well. I needed more of my mother and I was angry I was getting less and less of her as time went on.

My mother was only seventeen, when I was born. She knew nothing about mothering. I say this because she exerted no control over me, whatsoever. She let me take the lead and I gladly took it. I ran rampant over her and it left her bewildered. She must have felt so frustrated. In looking back at our times together, I wish she had had more experience with children. Then we might have had some chance of staying together.

My foster mother was the exact opposite. She had many years of caring for children. She was forty when I was born. Being from the old school, children were to be seen and not heard. She and I clashed often. If she said no, I said yes. I did not differ with her to cause any ruckus. I sincerely thought I was right and she was wrong. I don't know why. I did not openly oppose her. I did things my way as much as I could get away with behind her back. That way, I escaped punishment, at least for a while.

I knew all the differences between the two mothers and I loved them both. I did, however, play them against each other. Early on I knew my biological mother was not to be depended on, she was mostly for fun. Because that is what she and I would do, go out and have fun. We would go to the movies or the fair, whatever caught our fancy. But my foster mother was my shelter, my sustenance.

My foster mother would try to get me to talk about how I felt, when my mother would not show up, time and time again. But I would never talk to her about it. I was afraid my feelings were a betrayal against the woman who was always there for me.

My biological mother was called "Mama Dot," my foster mother was called "Mama." I called her mama because her house was full of children, all calling her mama. She had four daughters, and an adopted infant son. She also cared for infants from social services, who had become orphans for one reason or another. They stayed with us until they were adopted. I learned how to care for infants when I was a toddler. There were so many children, so everyone had to help care for them.

I remember one of the children was a little girl, named Martha Ellen. Her mother became ill and died. She stayed with us until she was adopted when she was four years old. She was a year older than I was and we were like sisters. I missed her presence a lot.

My foster mother stopped keeping the infants when I was about nine years old. It had been 3 years since we had heard from my mother. I guess my foster mother figured I was there to stay, if she let me. She was afraid the babies were distracting me from my school work. They probably did too, but so did everything else that I would have rather been doing.

Hide and Seek

As a very small child
I learned the word
Sad.
But sad seemed weak,
so I changed it to…
Mad.
Mad had more power,
more glory than
Sad.
Sad was wimpy,
not tough like
Mad.
Mad was the mighty lion,
while the little lamb was
Sad.
One day, I found myself
lost between the two.
I had to search long and hard
to separate who was who.
Then I gave up and cried
and faced that word
Sad.
To my surprise,
there was no more Mad.
And most of sad swept away.
So I made room for
Glad.

My Booga Man/Myself

Me and my booga man, we were tight.
He'd hide in my closet most every night.
I'd lay in my bed just a talkin' to him.
And tell him what a good booga man he'd been.
I guess I figured if I treated him right,
he might not eat me as a snack each night.
I made him lots of promises I could not keep,
wheelin' and dealin' tryin' to fall asleep.
Promised him birthday gifts I never got 'cause
I never found out when his birthday was.
What to get a booga man who has everything?
They hadn't come out yet with booga man rings.
So I praised him, and praised him, and praised him some more.
Perhaps he left 'cause he got plain bored.
Ya might think I'm crazy, the kindness I'd give.
But maybe that's why he let me live!
This is a true story, it happened just as I've said,
and it all took place inside my little head.

Discovery

Around the time I was entering my preteen years, I discovered some information, my grade school teacher had written in my permanent records. A close friend of mine, Pat, was staying after school a few times a week, completing some work she had missed while out sick. A couple of those times our teacher had gone home, leaving my friend alone in the classroom until her mother arrived to take her home. Pat decided she needed a break from the tedious school work. So she leaves her desk and begins wandering around our classroom. Her eyes became drawn to the teacher's file cabinets. She cautiously pulled open a drawer and to her surprise, stumbles upon the records of each class member. She felt delighted, I'm sure. She starts peeping through the files and pulls out her record. I do not recall what the comments said about her. I do remember, she did not agree with the analysis of herself and felt a bit angry. Then she goes further, pulling out my record. She reads it, laughs and carefully puts it back.

When Pat returns home, she gives me a phone call and tells me of her discovery. I listened to what our teacher had said about her, sympathetically. I could hardly wait to hear what was written about me. She wrote I talked and played too much. Lastly, she says, "Charlotte is just a free going, fun loving little girl." I was somewhat taken aback. She called me a "little girl." I didn't have a problem with the rest of it. After giggling, Pat and I said good-bye and hung up.

I thought about that one statement a lot, "free-going, fun loving". I decided it had a nice ring to it. I liked it. Ok, I thought, it's me! After that, from time to time, when I was in question of myself, I would think of that description and settle on it. It seemed to bring a pleasant and okay analysis of me to myself. It really *rocked* in my head! I became ...

Guilt 101

Well it'll hit you once
and it'll hit you twice,
those guilt trips hit you
all your life.

You can be working
or going to bed,
guilt don't care,
you'll wish you're dead.

It might be from your Mama,
it might be from your Pa.
Or it might just be something
stuck in your craw.

Why that guilt is so sneaky
and guilt is so sly,
you won't know it's there and
you're on the lie.

It holds marriages together and
helps spoil your child,
and you think you're doing good
for a little while.

Husbands and wives
beat each other up
and then do nice things to
overrun each other's cup.

Ol' guilt keeps you running;
you think you're being brave.
Then it fools you right down
to an early grave.

You keep on denying,
finding easy ways out,
'cause you're scared to ponder and
see what it's about.

You probably sinned
as a ten year old,
still you keep it buried deep
while you slowly grow cold.

You're scared to admit it,
ya think ya got to pay,
we forget Jesus did that
in His great day.

So pray hard about it,
and give it to Him.
Whatever you do,
don't take it back again!

If the Lord forgives you,
you ain't got the right,
to keep guilt with you
the rest of your life.

I've seen a lot of troubles
in my time and life,
many times there seemed
no end to my strife.

I never had it all,
but guilt, I never missed.
My guilt was so bad
it made me write this!

Sing Out

When I was 17 years old, in high school, I got an invitation that changed my life. A good friend of mine, Joyce Wilson, now Joyce Wilkerson, asked me to come with her that evening after school, to a singing group she was in, called Sing Out South. They were performing in a civic organization, of some sort. I had never heard of such a group and went out of curiosity.

I sat there in an auditorium and watched for Joyce to come on stage. The seats started filling up with the rest of the audience, there to see the show. The sound equipment was all set up, the guitar players were tuning their instruments, and the drummer was adjusting his drums.

Then it all got very quiet and the band started putting out fast and jazzy, upbeat music, and vocals. In only 1 or 2 beats of the music, youth came bursting forth and running, from the back of the auditorium, down through the four aisles. They ran past me yet orderly and uniformly, climbed up on the bleachers, clapping, smiling and singing with the band!

There was my friend, Joyce, in the back row, easily seen because she was tall. She was smiling and singing her heart out! They sang songs called; What Color is God's Skin, Freedom isn't Free, Joan of Arc, The Ride of Paul Revere, Up With People and many more. All of their songs were about love and acceptance of people and our differences. Many songs were about freedom and liberty for everyone. They sang words full of hope, telling us we can each could do our part, and make a difference in this world.

I was hooked and I wanted in! This group of people

was the first to ever inspire me with knowing I could make a difference. Lucky for me, a great singing voice was not required! They wanted our spirit and inspiration, and they got mine.

Amazingly, my mother let me join and hang with them. We sang almost every weekend, in any school, church, or organization that would let us in. We traveled all over Virginia in an old school bus, with the slogan, Sing Out South, on both sides.

We were a group of youth, aging from 17 to 20 plus years. Three to four of our parents served as chaperons for each trip. Our leader was Ines Thurston. Her husband, Ralph, drove the bus.

We were no particular domination of faith. We didn't do any preaching other than sharing the love of God. We were all colors, ages, backgrounds and income ranging from rich to poor.

When we sang together, we became a singular force to help produce hope, peace and harmony for all. As I traveled with Sing Out, I learned their history of how they were fashioned after the international Up With People cast, in Hollywood.

They had a rich history, dating back in 1965 when turbulence was world wide. The United States and Russia were back and forth about atomic weapons. Vietnam was deeply dividing everyone, including our youth. On top of it all, we had great racial strife dividing us even more.

Many university student presidents were so worried, they had a meeting to decide how they could come up with a positive way for college students to have their say.

They decided on a summer youth conference in Mackinac, Michigan, where they invited thousands of young people from all over the country. The mission was to come up with exactly, "What it was they wanted to see," as an answer to the strife. These young people decided to use music as their medium, and they put together in song, their best answers to help solve the world's problems.

From their very first show, a fire was lit. It sparked hope and enthusiasm that backfired into many more shows, as well as birthing new Sing Out groups all over the United States and many other countries as well. The national cast from Hollywood has traveled and performed in most countries around the world and are still going strong. In 2015, they introduced The Up With People anniversary show, titled, The Journey.

I lost touch with the Richmond Sing Out South when shortly after I finished high school and began working and then married. When I thought of doing a Sea Thru to You post on them, I Googled the national cast of Up With People. Wonderful memories came flooding back, as I watched the video of them singing the old songs.

I could see from the picture, the group members were exuberant and excited to share their message of hope. I think all the cast members felt that same great delight, each and every time we ran down aisles and up onto the bleachers to Sing Out!

Doctors

I wrote this poem
on a doctor's bill.
Truly I was hoping
he would cure my ills.

I think he should
charge me
one-half price,
without a guarantee to
save my life.

Perhaps I'll send it back
addressee unknown,
'cause all I've got
is what is shown.

So, what he'll get
is what you see.
I can't pay him
and he can't cure me.

"Excuse me, sir,
but I'm quite believing,
seems to me, Doctor,
that we're even!"

Smokin'

{'74-92}

Well I must admit,
though it hurts my pride,
I love carbon monoxide!
It just ain't enough to breathe fresh air,
I'd prefer there be some poison there.
I gotta have carbon monoxide.

First thing in the morning, when I wake up,
before I grab my coffee cup,
I light up carbon monoxide.
The very last thing at night I do,
when I'm tuckered out, tired and through,
I puff on carbon monoxide.

Well, I'm no alcoholic
and I don't do dope,
but I must admit, I'm engulfed in smoke.
Maybe I'll grab me a big Mack truck,
just ta see how well the exhaust pipe sucks,
and get plenty of carbon monoxide!

The Blood

In my latter 30's, I switched from being a receptionist, at the Richmond SPCA to a phlebotomist, at Virginia Blood Services. They took me untrained, as well as a few others, and taught us the basics of health care, screening of blood donors, blood collection and the after care of our potential blood donors. But to me, the most important thing I was taught there was the basic make up of our blood, itself.

When I would tell friends and family about my new occupation; most would respond very negatively. "Yuck, why are you playing in blood?" "Won't it make you sick, seeing people's blood?" "You're gonna stick people with a 16 gauge needle? Are you nuts, you don't know nothing 'bout taking blood!" That was true, I didn't. But something in me wanted to know. The more I learned about the whole process, the more I wanted to know about the whole process. It never repulsed or scared me. It did scare me if a donor felt lightheaded while donating or afterwards. I would take on their symptoms and feel like falling in the floor myself, all the while assuring them they were fine and would feel much better shortly. I laid them back with their head down and feet up and then placed an ice pack under their neck. I also prayed for us both … a lot.

The very word, blood, may sound disgusting to some. But to know all the wonders of it transforms it to majestic. The stuff is royalty. It runs freely through our entire body, feeding and nourishing it. It can heal our body and/or itself. Blood replenishes and cleans itself, as well as stopping the loss of it from our bodies by clotting. It regulates our body's acidity {PH} level and our response to outside temperatures. It's a perpetually blooming miracle 24/7. Mankind can't duplicate it. We're trying. We have synthetic alternatives but to duplicate blood as a whole fluid ... we've not yet succeeded.

I was so impressed by what I had learned my blood did for me I even stopped smoking. I had been trying to quit for years. With my vivid imagination, I added tar and nicotine to my body's process of making up my blood. Nasty stuff, mixed in my white cells, red cells and platelets. Oxygen anyone? Yeah, I quit smoking!

God is so great. He gives us so many chances to get it right. He gave us this royal filling, housed in amazing flesh to keep it and carry it around in and all the while it is keeping us healthy and alive. We get the full package right from the start of our lives, from our very first breath of air. We begin regardless of whether we live for God or never give Him a second thought. We get the blood either way.

I remember an old hymn I love, called, "I see a Crimson Stream." The refrain goes, "I see a crimson stream of blood, it flows from Cavalry. Its waves that reach the throne of God are sweeping over me."

Bad Day

Stop this world, I want it to stop,
stop this world and turn back the clocks.
Stop all the sadness, stop all the tears,
stop all the spoils and all wasted years.
Stop hungry children, stop sickness too.
Stop lonely old folks with nothing to do.
Stop unemployment, stop the welfare,
and stop all the lines till nobody's there.
Stop all the prejudice and stop all the hate.
Stop all the answers that hit us too late.
Stop all the farms with nothing to grow;
stop imports and exports with nowhere to go.
Stop all abortion, stop all the drugs;
stop sweeping evil under the rug.
Stop this world, I want it to stop.
Now stop this world and turn back the clocks!

Back to Buckroe Beach

Ever since I can remember, as a child, we went to Buckroe Beach, every summer. We always stayed a week. I accompanied my large, inherited family of 4 older sisters and 1 little brother. Mostly, I remember being there with my brother, Roger, and my next two older sisters, Linda and Julie.

We always stayed in the same little cottage, about two blocks from the beach front. I think there were a few motels/hotels back then but also lots of small cottages.

The one we rented had a screened-in front porch, two bedrooms, an eat-in kitchen, and only 1 bathroom. I remember, Mama saying it cost her from $100 to $150, for the week, back in the 1950's and 60's.

When we arrived, Mama and her sister, Aunt Florence, would scrub the entire cottage with Clorox bleach and water before allowing us to bring any of our stuff in. Wow, this was their vacation too?

Every day was spent pretty much the same way, the entire week, yet somehow, it made lasting, fond, fun memories for us all.

We would get up around 8:00, eat a big home-cooked breakfast, wash the dishes and put on our bathing suites. We'd grab a couple towels, and a couple old fashioned, tire inner tubes, then we'd walk the two blocks down to the beach.

Sometimes, Mama would let us rent a raft, to ride the waves. It was delightfully fun-me, Julie and Roger, trying to fit ourselves on the raft at the same time without turning it over! If we succeeded, it never lasted long, before we all tumbled off, but it was such fun trying to get on and stay on, even if only for a few moments.

When lunch time came, we'd grab the towels and tubes and walk back to the cottage to eat a good lunch and take a nap. We'd always take a nap. Because Mama and Aunt Florence needed the rest, well I guess they did!

After about an hour, or so, we'd put our bathing suits back on, get the towels and tubes, and walk back down to the shore for more fun in the water. We'd stay until early evening, splashing, floating and swimming in the water and playing in the sand.

Mama and Aunt Florence would each get in an inner tube and float out to about their waist, cause neither one of them could swim! They enjoyed just floating and talking with each other, as they watched us play.

Often, Roger and I would lie down on the sand and cover each other completely up with sand, except for our faces. This was particularly nice when we'd been in the water and were a bit chilly. The dry sand felt good and warm. We would pack each other down and it was fun to rise up afterwards, feeling the sandy-weight fall away and be free again.

When we were ready to eat supper we walked back to the cottage for another hot, home-cooked dinner. Mama and Aunt Florence were a real team in managing all of our activities.

After supper, we'd wash the dishes and put on clothes to go to the amusement park. We would set off again walking the two or three blocks to get there.

Back then, Buckroe had a wonderful amusement park. It seemed huge to me. It had everything an old fashioned park should have with lots of rides for children, teens and even adults. Linda and Julie were old enough to leave us and roam around together, unsupervised.

This park even had a gated stage and dance floor. There was a live band playing every night, except Sundays and Mondays. People would pay a quarter each to dance inside the gate, near the bandstand and would have to exit after each song then pay again for each song they wanted to dance to. No one danced outside of the gate.

Back then, the roller coaster was called The Dips. They also had an absolutely beautiful carousel, with horses and carriages. It played music from a pipe organ and drums that sounded delightful to me.

On our way out of the park, each night, my brother and I were allowed to "pull a string", pulling up a trinket toy, to walk back to the cottage with. Sometimes we stopped on the way and picked up a couple of comic books, to help put us to sleep, when we got in bed.

That's where we'd all go, too, as soon as we got back. Each day was very full, especially for Mama and Aunt Florence.

I remember lying in bed and listening to the hum of the park, still open, as I'd fall asleep. We were close enough to hear the Dips, and the carousel music, playing faintly, singing us to sleep.

Come the next day, we'd get up and do it all again, for a week. It was always a magical time of year and we always looked forward to going back the next year. There never seemed to be enough time with my family at Buckroe Beach.

We had our ups and downs there, like any family. Julie would complain because she had to share a bed with me. I would always get sand all in the sheets and she would get mad. Roger didn't want to ride the faster rides, when I wanted to. I was two years older and wanted to be tossed to and fro, way up and way down. He preferred the more gentle rides.

Funny, how families are fun and funny and drive each other nuts while all rolled into a family!

Some nights, when I can't sleep, I go back to Buckroe, in my mind. I relive the days, going back and forth and playing together, on our beach adventures, remembering different things at different times. Those were awesome days spent so long ago, you know? Then I fall asleep, as I go to the beach, just one more time.

Breaking Down

Woman, born a mate for man,
inferior to the rulers, who
decide what's best for me and you,
woman, start again and stand.

Woman, love yourself and then
shining forces help to feel,
showing through what's free and real.
Woman, love the world again.

Woman, born both black and white,
rising for the world to see,
unite our force and country,
woman, fight with love and light.

Woman, bind the love we sow,
ending hate, with love to give,
so our sons and husbands live.
Woman, mother's touch bestow.

To My Son, Jonathan At 12

As I watch you cross over, I remember lessons learned, replacing my ideals. I won't promise them to you. I can only practice daily. I refuse to let you down with the "perfect" setup. I'll try. I'll try not to possess you. You were only leant to me by God. It's hard to keep you free, and not see "me". I wish you to love yourself, as much as you love anyone else. I hope you have respect for the fine line dividing. That's the division and great war everywhere. I wish you balance there. If you can see and hear God in all people; you'll never be alone. And you'll never be too crowded. There's always room for one more heart. May your heart beat to God's drum, my son, Jonathan.

Jon at 12

Pipe Dreams

My head still spins a dream or two,
I thought I would outgrow.

There's one about my mother,
who left me years ago.

My mother stays and raises me,
she knows me very well.
She knows my every up and down,
the secrets I can't tell.

My mother sees through all my faults,
she's there through thick and thin,
we're not just a maternal bond,
we're also closest friends.

Sometimes we have a rift where we fight,
scream and shout.
But it does not take us anytime to forget
what it's about.

She loves me when I'm pure at heart
and when I play the sham.
Regardless if I'm right or wrong,
she loves me as I am.

But this is just a dream of mine,
my mother does not care.
She doesn't want to know me and
she's never, ever there.

I've feared I would be angry for as long as I live.
Yet, how could she give something
she'd never had to give?

So I'll just find a friend of mine,
and she will mother me.
And when she's down, if I'm around,
a mother is what I'll be.

My head still spins a dream or two,
I thought I would outgrow.
This one's about my mother,
who left me years ago.

Baby Face

I was lucky enough to work in a Child Development School, for a while, a few years ago. It was one of my most favorite and sweet experiences. When I'd come in, in the morning, I did not see a computer or a phone with 10 lines waiting on hold. I'd see tiny little faces all looking back at me, mostly smiling and happy to see me. My office was the toddler classroom. I was an assistant teacher to tiny boys and girls, age 10 to 16 months old. I feel very blessed to have kinda bumped into this position. I wasn't looking to be a toddler teacher, or any teacher for that matter. I took a position in the school's infant class, while one of their regular teachers was sick. She came back and I moved into another opening in this age classroom. I have enjoyed and learned so much from all our baby faces! They each have a magical way of stopping you in your tracks and making you smile, laugh, sing, dance, cry and making you love them.

One day I was down on the floor, as we are up and down a lot, watching one baby girl, as she was lying on her stomach. She was watching herself in the mirror, her little head bobbing up and down. Then she grew tired of that and started sucking on her forearm. I had to pick her up then. Wow, I never thought of calming myself that way! It's cheaper than Xanax. It doesn't destroy your liver like alcohol. Won't make you fat like junk food. I just keep forgetting to try it though.

I lost 20 lbs, the first year I worked there, without even trying. These little tiny people are just learning how to crawl, pull up on everything and artfully catch themselves so they don't fall. They are just learning to take their first steps and then they really feel empowered! Watch out then! We'd chase them daily, as they crawl, walk, run and interact with each other. They never heard of the word "share", and don't want to. Everything belongs to each one and each one wants everything right now, no waiting allowed! It's hysterical to watch, as they each discover their own emotions and feelings. As adults, we don't always understand our own, how can they understand theirs? Everything's new to them.

Mealtime, what a riot that is. Yep, we introduced them to sitting at their lil table, belted in their lil chairs. We give them plastic plates, filled with cut up food and sippy cups. Circus time, plates, cups and food are slid all over the lil table, the lil chairs, the lil people and the floor. Spaghetti is especially fun ... but that's how they learn. Practice makes perfect.

It's not all fun and games caring for these wee ones-it can quickly become overwhelming. They are sooo smart! They know when you are too outnumbered and they have the upper hand and they use it! I think, they have a built in radar for that. I swear they tag team each other, getting into mischief. They make every minute count. But that's part of their magic, they live in the moment. To keep up with them, we have to too. We often put on Naptime Symphony Music, to calm the teachers, way before naptime. Rainbow Fish is top on my list, "where's that disc, put it on please."

Children this age are just the most precious beings. They are so innocent and trusting, so honest and straightforward. They don't know to hide anything and don't care to. There's an old saying that children have special angels watching over them. I hope so. I wish every child to have at least 2 big angels, one on each side of them. It's an important position, watching over children this young. We introduce them to the world. We want them to feel loved and valued. We want them to grow up to love and value others. I love looking at those baby faces, and see the glee looking back at me.

Shelter

While I was still "the abandoned child"
and staying "lost" was still my style,
I decided to work awhile
at the Richmond S.P.C.A.

Well I couldn't believe how I fit in!
Didn't know whether to cry or grin,
my education was to begin
when I was 32.

I learned to purr, I learned to meow,
I learned to protect my home and growl!
Many times I felt the need to prowl,
but never jumped the fence.

It filled my voids to find them homes,
I weaned young orphans left alone.
Neglect and abuse were often shown;
so we preached on humane care.

And surplus animas was sure no bull,
as love was lost with each pet pulled.
I dreamed heaven was half past full,
great weight was ours to bear.

I cried and hurt for dogs and cats.
While many a night was spent like that,
my past and present were now at bat,
my heart became untied.

There was nothing left to do but deal.
Through their pain, it made me feel
and feeling mine just made me real.
The truth was now my own.

Those furry creatures made me see
that I had never cried for me.
Who would guess I'd be set free
by man's best friend?
Amen!

I Remember Mother

I hid from your pain for years,
but you were still there,
and nowhere.

People would tell me,
"You'll always feel some bad."
And again I'd get mad.

I want to be free,
without abandoning you,
but only for myself.

I try to tell you "Good-bye."
Because I will not try and find you.

It's still your turn,
and I'm still young again.
I think I'm kinda like you, but I have to go,
I never liked sad and it hurts now
but that's better.

Cat Rap

ATTENTION
HUMANS!
Or to whom it may concern.
Please listen to this
if you'd like to learn.
You've such high intelligence,
yet you misunderstand,
we feline beings were not made
to please Man!
If you think we should be like
"Man's best friend",
you should pause in your tracks,
and think again.
We don't come when called,
or when you feel the need.
We don't do commands,
and we will not retrieve.
We look nice on your furniture,
we look good in your chair.
And if that's where we pose,
you should leave us right there.
And cats are supposed to climb
EVERYWHERE!
We look great on the table,
we make an elegant centerpiece.
So don't scream your loudest
and toss us beneath.
You should stroke us real gentle
and please scratch our heads.

Move on over,
make more room in your bed.
Look at the world, Man,
change your ways.
You could take a lesson from Egyptian days!
They knew what was what,
and cats were the craze!
You've changed all this,
and computerized that,
but there's just no way
you'll ever change us cats.
Don't get so tangled up
in all your progress.
STOP! LOVE A CAT 'cause
cats love BEST!!!

Rhyming

Dear Father in heaven, please help me along.
Searching for peace, I've discovered I'm wrong.
I can rhyme any story, rhyme any line,
I see love out front and my heart stays behind,
I'm not rhyming.

How can I feel empty and yet feel so full?
Why still deny when my heart feels a pull?
My head's full of knowledge,
yet my mouth spits hate.
I brim with understanding
and still arrive late.
I don't rhyme.

I can't find my rhythm, keep missing the beat,
I keep rhyming off key and dropping the sheet.
Then I fumble my lyrics, feel bad and fall.
So I give up and cry and curse at it all.
I can rhyme any name, rhyme any word,
yet my own song is missing,
my own song's unheard.

I'm not rhyming,
Father where's perfect timing?
I don't rhyme.

About Summer Cat

This next poem is very small, yet so very large. There is no animal shelter big enough to build, that would house the enormous number of unwanted and indiscriminately bred cats and dogs. If you can see the big picture, this problem is everywhere. When I worked at the Richmond SPCA, we would receive 50 to 100 puppies and kittens in a DAY. This took place all summer, 5 days a week. There is no possible way to adopt them all out to new homes or have space to shelter them all.

Would you want to live your life in a small cage, day in and day out? It ruins their personalities, makes them very sad and unhappy. Our newer no kill shelters are great, but they have to turn animals away, due to lack of space. It is unbelievable what people will do to rid themselves of their beloved pet when they are desperate. Dogs and cats, kittens and puppies are dropped in the streets, in the woods and in the neighborhoods, like trash. They are even dropped in bags and boxes on busy highways. The ONLY answer is to spay and neuter all dogs and cats, until the number born is closer to the number of available homes. Yes, this will take time to accomplish. But we have to become more vigilant; in order to eliminate the horrible suffering of innocent, unwanted furry infants and babies.

Summer Cat Blues

Sometimes, it seems like
a thousand cats came in today.
Each one crying for a place to stay.

Our shelter is already overrun;
we curse the job that must be done.

Each year we hear the same old reasons,
we cope with this each summer season.

A million tears could fall in vain—
and still each summer remains the same.

Dear God,
teach people to neuter and spay—
a thousand cats came in today.

Remembering Shelter Days

While proofing my book, Shelter, it brought back memories of some of my days spent there. We would come in at 8:00 in the morning, all the dogs would be barking for breakfast. The cats would be restless, knowing food was on the way and their litter boxes were being cleaned. The phones would start ringing off the hook, I want a dog, I lost a dog, I found a dog ... The kennel staff cleaned and feed the furry guests, while the reception staff answered the phone and started talking to people about our adoption policies and such.

Also, we provided a lost and found service for the public. We had lists of pets misplaced and needing assistance. That used to drive me wild. People describe colors, sizes, breed, male and female, all different! This lead to a very difficult task of matching lost and founds pets. It was exceptionally great though, to reunite pets and their people.

Being there for 5 years taught me a lot about people. After you see the same people, bringing in litter after litter of unwanted babies, refusing to spay and neuter; it does something to you. This was done by educated and uneducated folks, alike. After a couple years, you start to notice some of the people adopting, were the very ones bringing pets back later, only to adopt a new puppy or kitten. Maddening ... to say the least, they did not really want a live pet. They wanted a baby to play with for a while. I often wished we could and would enforce tougher adoption rules. If you bring it back; you don't get another one.

We adopted each pet out with a certificate to spay or neuter, up front. Were they used and the animal never bred? Some were, some were not, or used after 1 or 2 litters of babies born.

While I was there, our staff had a great way of letting off steam and rolling with the pain and emotional turmoil in the atmosphere. When the public was not around, we would cut up and act crazy, sing, dance, make each other laugh hysterically. One of the kennel technicians, I'll call him Sam, would fall on the floor and pretend to wrestle this huge stuffed bear. He'd yell for help as if he was being eaten! Sometimes he would dance up on the long counter, pretending to hold a microphone while singing Bruce Springstein songs. We all got zany for a few moments. We had to, kind of like the TV program, Mash. We had to balance out the deep sadness of the place. It was the only way we could continue to stay there.

It's no wonder I had to come clean and face my own demons. It was too real and I guess I had to be too. I literally did dream heaven was half past full. I saw us sticking cats and dogs up there like it was a full attic with absolutely no more room. It was a nightmare come true every day. Summer, my favorite time of the year, carefree, fun summertime was the absolute pits. Cause we were stuffing mostly babies up into heaven.

I don't know how I stayed 5 years. But I do know I truly grew up there. Those animals changed my life. They helped me start the grieving process I had so long denied. I am hoping maybe this book might help change theirs for the better. What a wonderful world, where only a few shelters are needed. There is no euthanasia, no pets in cages for months or years. Every animal is loved and cherished. While I'm dreaming, there's no orphanages either. Every child born is loved and cherished, understood and kept forever. There's no broken homes, no lost love. Sounds like a dream? Ok, I'm dreaming it. That's a start.

Other Mothers

After you'd been gone awhile,
I went back to the child
you tried to rescue,
who had never understood
the distance between us.
But all the time you knew
and knew I didn't.
And me, being left behind,
what else could I do,
but slight you?
I guess my broken, baby heart,
hardened yours a little;
while you played second fiddle.

To Mama

I often wish, I could still talk to my deceased Mama. I refer to her as, Mama, because she was the one that mothered me. She was my first shelter and my rock to cling to. Mama, nor I, never knew when or if my biological mother would show up. I believe we both were filled with much anger and animosity about that. So I directed my anger on her; "She was not my mother." I greatly resented her. How ironic of me! But that's the child and I believe that response takes place often in broken parent/child relationships. Hind sight is 20/20, sad that it is, huh? Yes, I would most certainly like to talk to Mama again. God has given me a few healing dreams of this. We meet in heaven and embrace and both of us apologize profusely. I love that dream.

Gifts of Joy

Before I knew
the joy of You,
I thought my soul would never fill.
You died for every sin
I could ever commit,
I could not accept it.
Still, the Holy Spirit keep
prompting me,
waiting only for me to prompt.
Through only Your grace, I am perfect
in God's sight,
though I will never be just right.
And just as I am now, You're here
to see me through.
My dearest Jesus,
I thank You.

Bye-Bye Baby

It is an exciting time, working in a child care center. There's never really a dull moment. My class consists of 1 year old toddlers, and they are so much fun. They are just coming into their own, discovering their little selves, their temperament, feelings and personalities.

They have so much to teach us, it astounds us daily. Their eyes and ears see and hear it all. They don't miss a trick, don't think they do!

One of the most important time of the day for them, in all their new found behaviors and feelings; is when it's time for Mom or Dad to come pick them up.

If mom or dad, is consistent enough, in coming around the same time every day; they Know it. They sense when it's time for their parents to come.

Our classroom is lucky enough to have full view of the parking lot and the road that leads into it. So we use the windows to look for mom or dad, they love to do this! If one child goes up to the window; 2 or 3 go with them. It can have a calming effect on them, if they are getting antsy or whining for their parents to come get them.

They learn to wave "bye-bye" in our class, and blow kisses, for the first time. They love to wave to their friends leaving and see and wave at the parents coming up the sidewalk to get the other kids!

But they can also get upset, seeing their friends get picked up and their parent has not come yet. I think they feel left out and maybe feel a tinge of abandonment or fear.

Usually there is almost always one little toddler left alone, no other little friends, no parents, for a few minutes.

It is not unusual to have to stop any cleaning you might be trying to get done and spend time with that one lone child.

They will let you know it too. Suddenly there they are at your feet, looking up at you with a sad lil lonesome look or whimpering for you to hold them.

I pick them up and whisper in their ear; "Mommy/ Daddy's coming in a minute, they will be here." I take them over to the window and we sit and look for them. We look at each car to see if that is them or not, "Nope that's not them!"

After a few minutes, that gets boring for the child and I have to carry them to the door. Ours is a divided door and so you can see out and keep the children in, at the same time. They love to sit on the top of the bottom part of the door, while looking down the hall for mom or dad.

At that big moment, their parent arrives; everything is Right with the world! They are all smiles and jump into their arms. It is so great to see their parents appreciate their child's glee at seeing them, at last! Many parents comment; "That's the best time of their day, when they see their child smile and be excited and happy to see them."

We might get a wave goodbye from each child, or a kiss blown from their little hands. We might even get ignored, cause now we are chopped liver. Bye-bye, Baby!

Cat Tales

Orange tabby, Tom
and Ching a male Siamese cat,
were both homeless strays engaged in a spat.
There was fur everywhere, and loud catawauling.
They were hissing and spitting, there was growling
and mauling.

They took a short break to see who was ahead
and orange tabby, Tom angrily said,
"This is my territory, where I like to roam,
I strongly suggest you find a new home."

As he cautiously preened, appearing quite calm
Ching the Siamese said to orange tabby, Tom,
"Why don't we just share?
It's a big neighborhood."
"Stop playing the bully and see if we could."

Tom flattened his ears, and let out a low yowl.
Then his eyeballs grew big as he started to growl,
"I ain't gonna share, so get ready to run,
whether you know it or not,
your life's about done."

Ching stood arched and ready, not moving an inch.
Then his brain started ticking while his eyes
did not flinch.
"I really admire you, Tom, all on your own,
it's still new to me, living alone."

Well, Tom felt a bit flattered,
so he backed up a bit.
He really couldn't believe this Siamese twit!
"The street's all I know,
I've always roamed this way.
My Pa was a fierce fighter, my Ma was a stray."

Ching felt a surge of pity
for the crude orange feline.
He figured conversing
would buy himself more time.

"You could take over some people,
let them wait on you.
Don't work like a dog
your whole life through."

"Oh, come on", said Tom with a grimacing scowl,
"You domesticated cats
shouldn't be allowed to prowl.
It's wimps like you that give cats a bad name,
your pussy-footing ways bring
disgrace and shame."

Ching swallowed hard, determined to save face.
At the same time, getting himself out of that place.
"Education and refinement are certainly no crime.
It would be a nice change
from the fleas, dirt and grime."
Just then something moved
and caught old Tom's eye.
Under his breath he breathed a deep sigh.
"It's lucky for you, I gotta go.

I've been waiting for weeks
to meet that young Calico."

The Tom cat dashed off,
the Siamese was saved by love!
He sighted with relief
and thanked the heavens above.

As he straightened himself up,
and jauntily started to go,
a big pink Cadillac drove by very slow.

Ching quickly plopped down,
looking helpless and lost,

while he pitifully meowed
with a sputtering cough!
Sure enough the pink Cadillac took him away,
and he hasn't seen Tom again to this very day!

Red Flags

Beaches are just the best places in the world to me. As a child, I went with my family I had inherited, every summer to Buckroe Beach. Those times are some of my fondest memories. So I am a water person. Because of this and my love for adventure; I had to grow a fear, or respect of the ocean water. After I was grown, I spent a few years without visiting a beach. But when I returned, boy did I make up for lost time. I have had some exciting vacations learning respect for the water.

One big lesson took place at Virginia Beach. I was with my lifelong friend, Candace and her son, Thomas Preston or TP. It was just our luck to be there during a rip tide. Wouldn't you know it we had just purchased a new raft for the waves. We get down to the beach and there are red flags everywhere, lifeguards alert and watching. But, people were swimming. Kids were playing in the water. So we jump into the wild and swirling waves! Funny thing, as we were all three experienced water/beach people, we failed to fully realize that the tide was going out.

Yeah, we got caught, swirling and drifting out to Never Never Land. We knew we were in real trouble when we could not touch the ocean bottom with our feet. The lifeguards whistled several times but we couldn't get back. So, one of them came out, with his little red, floaty thing, to save us. He was young and muscular, praise God. TP was on the raft and Candace was in the water, but hanging on to it. I was trying to catch a hold of it but not succeeding. The lifeguard grabbed on and started towing them in. But

I could not get a hold. I struggled and struggled, while the water just kept trying to drag me farther out.

Candace became really concerned and continuously called for me to catch up with them. All I could do was keep paddling towards them, fighting against the pull of the water moving out. After much effort, I did catch a hold and was dragged to safety along with them. We were made to stay on the beach for thirty minutes for our punishment of going out so far.

It seemed funny then, because we did not mean to get swept up and go out that far. It just happened. But later, I kept recalling the incident, mentally re-enacting it. I realized even a second lifeguard might not have had time to get to me before I was pulled under, or ran out of breath and energy. I had never had to struggle that hard before in the water to save myself. That's when I scarily knew I really could have drowned.

I had never been afraid in the water before 'till then. Even during it, when the lifeguard was coming out to us and then pulling them in, I wasn't thinking, " I'm gonna drown and die." My mind automatically went into survival mode. I guess it was more like " grab that raft". Now I wonder, what if I was consumed with fear and the possibility of drowning and not focused on survival. Would I have been able to catch the raft? I never thought about that till writing this post. Hind-sight's 20/20. We just wanted to have fun at the beach. How easily the tide does change things. I won't ever be as adventuresome, in the water, as before that beach trip.

I am reminded of the Bible story of Jesus walking on the water in Matthew 14:25-31. One of His apostles, Peter asked to walk on the water also. At first he did, walking towards Jesus. But when he saw the "wind boisterous, he was afraid" and began to sink. He cried out to the Lord to save him and Jesus did. Peter fell because he moved his focus from Jesus, to the wind and water.

Each spring I can hardly wait for summer and beach time. But after that adventure, I know to focus on safety first and then have loads of fun.

Father Is

I am the A, I am the Z,
come to me.
I am the beginning, I am the end.
I am now, I was then.
Come to me.
I am gentle, I am mild,
you can see me in a child.
I'm in the young, I'm in the old,
I'm in the meek, I'm in the bold.
I am always everywhere,
and in everything I care.
I love to laugh, I love to sing.
I love every living thing.
Every soul that is of me;
will know my love and be set free.
I was
I am
I will be,
Come to me.

I Am

Have you ever wondered about any of the Old
Testament Bible stories? Some of them seem really
far out and removed from modern times. I pondered
the great story of Moses, from the book of Exodus.
Moses prays to God. God tells him to go tell the
Pharaoh in Egypt, to let His people go. He tells
Moses to lead the Israelites, in their expedition to
freedom. Moses responds by arguing with God.

"Who am I, to lead the children of Israel?"

Interestingly, God didn't tell him who he was.

He didn't say Moses would be famous and
go down in history. Instead, he said, "Surely
I will be with you." A flabbergasted Moses
asked, "Who do I tell them has sent me?"

"I AM THAT I AM. You tell them I AM sent you."

Poor Moses must have had an adrenaline rush with
that statement! Surely, if he'd had access to some
Xanax, he might have popped one or even two!
None the less, with his brother, Aaron's help, he lead
the children of Israel as the Lord asked him to.

God was with him then and God is with us
now. He is the Great I AM, that still is.

He's right here anytime we have a need, waiting
for us to heed Him. He still does miracles, healing
bodies, changing hearts, minds and lives. He
gives to us daily, our daily bread, but I've been
thinking, He also must want it back. He wants
us to be I AM for Him, again and again.

What father, mother, sister, brother, friend or lover
wouldn't want it back? I bet, He isn't interested in our
"shoulda, coulda, woulda's." He already knows all our
different circumstances, like Moses. Isn't it perfectly
right for Him to want us to give back to Him?

Doesn't that really mean giving to "who-so-ever" needs
us daily, moment to moment? In the New Testament book
of Matthew, Jesus comforted His disciples, saying, "Lo,
I AM with you always, even until the end of the world."

I AM always with you.

So, Heaven help me be I AM for Jesus. Is there
any greater commission for Christians?

In Church

Sitting in church today,
I judged my brother.
With a glance he never saw,
I built a wall, gloriously tall,
between his heart and mine.
But then, the Lord stepped in.
He showed me my brother's childlike self,
denied something way back when.
And he simply had to act it out again.
I couldn't help but feel akin.
Glory Hallelujah!

Spca Christmas

A few nights before Christmas at the SPCA,
the staff had gone home, when I decided to stay.
We had pets still unwanted and I felt very bad.
With no home for Christmas,
I knew they'd be sad.
I crept down the corridor with a quiet slow walk,
when suddenly I heard
the dogs reminisce and talk!

"I remember", said the collie, "This time last year,
when I never dreamed I'd ever by here.
I even had presents under the tree.
I had a big family, all loving me."

"Me too," cried the bulldog, whimpering low.
"But my family said I was too big and must go.
Last year I was just a fat little pup.
Now I've lost it all, just by being grown up."

Rusty, the terrier, was one of our strays,
he'd been waiting to be found
with each passing day.
"I was hit by a car and my legs became lame.
I thought I was a goner till that rescue truck came."

"A humane officer freed me",
said the Doberman called Bones,
I was tied to a chain, forgotten and alone.
My family used me to help keep them safe,
while I often dreamed of being free, like a waif."

The cats were all talking and meowing too.
Some were pawing the cage bars,
trying to get through.
A big ole alley cat, whose name was Tom,
was happy to be here and felt no alarm.

"Why I never had such fine tasty meals,
after rummaging trashcans, this food is unreal!
I spent many a night, freezing and wet.
This has just got to be the best home yet."

"I quite disagree," said the Siamese, named Ming.
I had a huge house, and I ran the whole thing.
I kept everyone hopping and under control.
I still can't believe this is where I'll grow old!"

"A-Choo!" sneezed the big fluffy Persian
named Mic,
"I'm lucky they gave me an antibiotic!
I was sick with a flu and very close to death.
If it wasn't for these people,
I'd have breathed my last breath."

I heard every pet; they shared one by one.
They told of their lives and what they had done.
By then, it was late and I knew I must leave.
I knew I had heard what no one would believe!

While closing the door,
the old Shepherd named King,
called out to the rest, "Let me tell you something.
Be thankful for our shelter, let's stop all our fuss.
The staff asked for donations
and hung stockings for us."

"I've lived a long time, so believe what I say.
There will come for us all, a much better day.
Somehow MAN will help make our lives
turn out right.
Merry Christmas to you, and to us all,
A good night!!"

1955 - Charlotte Ann and Santa

Still There

Around 1991 or 1992, I had been gone from the SPCA, maybe about a year or two; I saw a commercial on the TV, on animal abuse. Immediately, that heartbreaking old pain reappeared in my chest. I had never missed it until then. Feeling the brokenness and hurt from it again, I suddenly remembered and realized I had felt the same pain, the 5 years I worked at the shelter. It had become a part of me and I had let it hurt me all that time. Somehow, it had become a physical habit I had just unconsciously decided to live with while working there. I did not even know when it had temporarily left or that it did leave, until I left the shelter and been gone awhile and saw the commercial on abuse and neglect. I'm not sure I consciously knew it was there, while I worked at the shelter. It had to be numbed, in order to sustain my work for the animals. If I felt a pain, such as that magnitude, what in the world, did the cats and dogs feel? Our staff knew the animals could sense and smell death when they were brought through the door. Their owners and caretakers would leave them in a strange place, alone and abandoned. Most of them never saw their beloved people again. If the animals ever knew love again, it was from curious strangers, giving them a second chance at life. They had been left once, at least. Would the new family abandon them also, after their guard was down and they had fallen in love again? I would guess, the fur babies feel the same feelings step and foster children feel, as the family falls apart. But like babies, they have no voice. Bigger shelters is not the answer. We must neuter and spay diligently, until the number of cats and dogs is somewhere closer to the number of available homes for them. We must find a way to stop the breeders, as well. We must find a way to stop this atroscious problem, for our furry friends. I believe our Creator loves His animals, because He made them. I don't believe it was ever His intentions for any animals or any living creature, to suffer abuse, at the use of mankind. Certainly, it was His intention for them to live life on this planet, unharmed and appreciated by His people, He set over them. What are we going to do? The cages are still full. The shelters are still overrun. Fur babies are still waiting for us to figure it out. Days go by, weeks, months, then years and they are still there.

One Stanza

So many years
spent in hiding.
So much energy
spent denying.
When all I wanted
was what I should have had.
Just love
and attention
from my Dad.

Conference

Look what I've done
in that ding-dang rhyme.
I gave my Father
one lousy line!

You'd think I could make him
just a little more space.
But no, I robbed him
of his place.

Do ya' think perhaps
I'm on the run?
Did I shoot that man
with his very own gun?

Is this love or is it war?
What'd I have to do
that for?

Well the words kinda slipped
through my fingertips.
'Cause they never quite made it
across my lips.

'Cause I never got to be
"Daddy's Girl."
With this mo-chine,
I thee hurl!

I don't want the battle,
I want the whole war,
and this is what
I'm writing for.

The Child

While I worked at the Child Development School in 2015, I knew I had come full circle. I started life in a group of children and here I was surrounded again by infants and toddlers. I loved working with them and they loved me too. Watching them daily, as they interacted with the teachers and each other, helped me look back at my toddler self, long ago. I could fully appreciate how confused and angry I had felt, being forgotten and abandoned.

I loved to watch the toddler's expressions and see how they reacted to the other children, as well as the teachers. I learned how detrimental it is to them to be cared for by people who are happy and love caring for them. They don't understand a bad day, or that we feel sick or tired or worried about our personal lives. They understand our faces, if we smile, laugh or frown. They hear our voice, if it is soft and kind or sharp and impatient. If the person caring for them is uninterested and really wants to be somewhere else, they sense it. That shuts them out, so-to-speak. They internalize that behavior and learn to shut us out as well. They take it personal, that something is wrong with them. That's the way they think at that age, everything is about them.

I was really impressed when I visited the 3 and 4 year old class. There, they teach them about their feelings and how to manage them. The class room had set up different sets of boards for the kids. The first board listed all the children's names. The children would come in and mark that they were present beside their name. Then they would move on to a board that held Feeling Blocks. These were labeled happy, sad, mad, or frightened and so on. They would then choose the block that described how they were feeling and place that block beside their name, on the Roll board. That way, everyone could see how they felt. It also assisted the child in knowing and labeling their different feelings. Next, there was a board set up with blocks, each listing different ways they could make themselves feel better. That was their next task, to choose a block, they thought might help them, that particular day, such as, read a story, paint, and so on. Then later in the day, the teachers would discuss with them and the class, whether those things they chose and did, helped or not. If not, they would choose another block and try again. If they chose a block saying they felt good, they got to tell the class why it was a good day for them, thus far. This helped the child in learning to help themselves in feeling better. I think this method also helped them learn and practice making choices and having a say, as to what they participated in, each day. It put some control into their little hands, and who doesn't like that?

As an adult, I have worked in businesses that could have used this method to assist their employees! How often have we not identified our own feelings and made terrible choices because of them? I should have learned this when I was 22, I might have made better choices then, instead of bumbling along every day!

I am so glad we, as human beings, have learned to assist children at a very young age, in understanding themselves, being human.

Grown Son

Now and again, I dream of him.
He's in my arms, and I smell his
sweet familiar baby scent.
And the feeling of having him nestled next to my skin,
where no harm can get in.

But now he's grown and out there; nestled in the city,
with angel's arms holding him.
How often I feel I've messed up the rhyme,
so often I fear we will run out of time.

Clyde the Camel

Clyde is a homeless camel. He was abandoned by his owner, Ibinabum, the Arab. Ibinabum ditched him because he did not want a dirty old camel trashing his home. Poor Clyde wound up in an animal shelter where he didn't fit in. All the cats and dogs made fun of him. He was the first and only camel they had ever seen! They made rude comments about his hump back and hurt his feelings. Clyde was so sad, having to live every day with such abuse. He really is no trouble to care for. He has such a sweet disposition and is trained to a litter box. Although he does require a larger pan than cats and dogs; as camel droppings are considerably bigger than dog poo! Plus, camel poo makes great fertilizer and you get exotic vegetables from it in your garden! An entire room will suit him nicely.

All this could be yours...

So this is the plea, you adopt Clyde and let him live with you in your home; safe and secure with people that understand what it's like to be different.

If you would like to adopt him just check the appropriate box and sign on the dotted line and Clyde can be yours forever!

#Yes, I'll keep Clyde forever
#No, Why would I want a smelly, ole' camel?

Animal Life

We, as human beings, have the biggest need of food, to feed our planet, than ever before. It is so very sickening to me, to hear and see the abuse and use of our cows, pigs, chickens, lambs and all the living creatures we use for food.

They are now mass produced, fed antibiotics and steroids, for excessive growth for consumption. Many are taken away from their mothers too soon. They are kept in unhealthy, extremely cramped and very uncomfortable cages and pens. They are horribly overcrowded, treated and handled with contempt and even hatred.

Long ago, we needed their fur and hide to keep warm and protected from the elements. But not now, we have many other avenues of manufactured materials for this. Still, many people desire their fur and feathers, as a sign of their prestige and glamor. Many animals and fowl are cruelly ripped of their bodily coverings while they are still alive.

Many creatures are tortured before they slowly die. It's as if their caregivers delight in seeing the animal's pain and agony.

How did we as human beings grow to such a lowly level of behavior towards living creatures? Where has kindness and compassion gone? What is causing people to react in such cruel and vicious behavior towards God's creatures?

We must find a way to stop this madness. It is a form of madness too. It's as if we are trading places with the beasts. Are we becoming beasts ourselves?

Heaven help us find the answers for stopping this crude and abusive behavior. A great number of people have become vegetarians, in response to this overabundance of animal manufacturing. I don't know the answer to this problem. I pray God will hear our prayers and give us the answer. Please pray and search for ways to combat this horrific abuse of our animal friends, Amen.

Daddy

When I heard you had died, for so long I did not cry.
Instead I told myself great big lies.
The lies helped me forget,
much later I wept.
I heard you went down with an unfair fight.
For neither of us, had it turned out right.
I was gonna find you and show you my
wonderful son,
we could have made up for what you hadn't been
or done, together.
For so long I wanted you, Daddy,
but I cast no blame.
The tears and great rains, finally came.
So I'm saving you lots of hugs and kisses,
for all of those years and all of those misses.
I miss you too, Daddy.

War

Lord, I want to help you,
You know I really do.
If You would just get me over myself,
and set me free for You.

Can't help that I'm American,
taught to have it my own way.
But when I look in Your Good Book,
I see something gone astray.

My ego is just busting to
express my selfish side.
Yet, Jesus says to
turn my cheek and
swallow all my pride.

My inner child is screaming,
she wants to act it out.
If I let her have her way
that's not what You're about.
I start with good intentions,
all Your ways are on my mind.
Then I want,
and I need
and I feel
and I know
and I've taken up
all Your time.

There's this sneaky "switch-off" button
hiding somewhere in my head!
When I try and concentrate on You,
it switches to me instead!
Lord,
shake me,
wake me,
spin or win me,
slip and slide me there.
Do you think it would help me stay
on You if I just stayed in prayer?
Lord, I want to help You.
You know I really do.
If you would just get me over myself
and set me free for you!

Loving One Another

A few summers ago, I helped my friend with her Christian Camp, Camp Grace. She needed a cabin leader for the youngest girls. I had great trepidation, I was in my 60's, but I agreed to help her.

So we had 10 little girls in one small cabin. They ranged from 4 yrs. old to 7 or 8 years old. There was 1 other person helping, and she was in charge, thank You, Jesus. I was to assist her. We had 10 different tiny little ladies, all from different backgrounds, ready to have some fun!

I noticed one particularly quiet girl, about 7. She had no pajamas, a sundress, a pair of jeans, a pair of shorts and a bathing suit. No one had really packed for her and so that was what she came with for a week. Her name was Star. It bothered me that she was withdrawn and kept to herself. I tried to draw her out and get her excited and interested in the activities for each day. Something in me felt a burden for her. Slowly, Star began to respond and come alive a bit.

She had an older sister and an older brother there, in their own age group. When we ate meals, we all ate together. When she saw her older sister in the mess hall, she'd come alive beaming with proud exuberance, declaring, "That's my sister!" But to my dismay, her sister shunned her and verbally put her down. I sat there watching Star's countenance fall, with her little head slowly bending down, eyes following, in shame and pain. The whole scene hurt my heart, as if I was the one shunned. To make matters worse, her older brother followed suit. Again she'd beam with pride seeing her big brother, proudly saying the same thing, "That's my big brother!" He shunned her and pretended he never saw her, looking over her head. As before, her sweet little countenance would fall as her head fell in shame. I watched this for a week.

Towards the end of the week, I found myself talking to Star when she was alone. Trying to explain to her 7 year old self, how her sister and brother did not really hate her. I explained they were just caught up in their own struggles of life and they would perhaps treat her better as they grew out of their self-centeredness. Her reply was; "They don't care about me." How could I blame her for that feeling?

Thinking about it later, it dawned on me, I had done the same thing to people I loved, when we were very young. The next question was, why? It was actually the same thing I told her, that's where I got it from. I was so caught up in my own pain of being abandoned by my biological parents; I took my anger for them and projected it on the ones that loved me. It never occurred to me then that I might be breaking tender little hearts, hurting someone's countenance. How many had I so carelessly hurt the same way? Certainly, I had often seen this behavior before, in other people's siblings. But it struck home this time at camp, watching Star be wounded over and over again.

The most important thing Jesus commanded us to do was to, "Love One Another." Sounds so very simple and is obviously so very difficult to accomplish. I bet we fail every day, at work, at home, with someone.

It seems the ones we fail the most are our own loved ones. How absurd is that? It's a bitter, ugly cycle of dysfunctional love, passed down to us from our parents and other important people in our lives who taught us to love. They have the same story. Their parents passed it down to them and so on. But the buck has to stop somewhere, with someone willing to stop it. When we don't stop destructive behavior, we become it. We have to catch ourselves, in the heat of the moment and with emotions flying. Easy, not hardly! It does get easier over time, with practice and determination. We make new habits of behavior. We have to do the work, over and over, to change. But more importantly, we begin to follow God's instructions. Yes, He could zap us into obedience. But He has always given us free will to be what we choose to be. I think a lot of times, He chooses to let us struggle and do the work. Then it really means more to us and becomes our testimony. Anything is always worth more if we have worked hard for it. Jesus, help us learn to love one another, Amen.

Diamonds

Diamonds falling from our eyes,
shall we let the truth arise?
Such a most expensive call,
should we let these jewels fall?
Ah, to see the clearer view,
both of me and of you.
Can we see the hidden price,
love held hostage, or more abundant Life?

Fur Boy

A few years ago, I lived out in Ruther Glen, Virginia, back in the woods and off the main roads. My house was surrounded by trees and woods on all sides. It sat about 100 feet off the road. There was an acre of wooded land on both sides of my house and more than that in the back of it. I loved it there. I got to help all sorts of little critters! I rescued baby birds, a baby squirrel, a baby rabbit, a puppy and a few expectant female cats and their newborn kittens. My son was grown, working and living in Richmond. So except for a few sparse neighbors, and the little country church I attended there, I was alone with just the animals.

One warm 4th of July, I was trying to leave and go to my sister, Julie's house, in Chesterfield, where our family was celebrating the holiday.

All of a sudden, I hear a kitten desperately crying, as if for his mother! I was all too familiar with that terrified, pitiful baby scream. I look out the back door and there's this bright orange kitten looking back at me, lost and scared. He looked to be about 7 or 8 weeks old and a bit thin. I head towards him and he runs under my deck. I try a couple more times to catch him, but he's too fast.

Then I decide, maybe he will calm down if I sound more like a kitten, myself. I started meowing in a high pitch voice. At first, he almost fell for it. But then he took off again running around my house. So here I am, running after him, meowing like a crazy woman, chasing this baby! I was really glad the woods were in full bloom and nobody was able to view this spectacle.

The 4th of July was ticking by, so I gave up chasing

him. I set a bowl of cat food under the edge of my back deck and took off to Chesterfield.

When I returned home, he was there. I was so relieved. I had thought and worried about him all day. I moved the bowl of food closer to my back door, on my deck. I was afraid for this baby to be out in the woods alone. Several times at night I would check on him. He would be asleep on the railing of my deck. I tried every day to catch him. I started leaving a bowl of food out for him daily. He grew a bit friendlier after a couple days. He let me get closer to him, but still ran if I made a move to grab him. I had every intention of trapping him in my house and domesticating this 'lil fur ball.

One morning, I just knew I was gonna catch him that day. I plotted it all out. I moved his food right next to my back door, with the door open. I stayed close by and watched him eye me cautiously. I slowly moved in, inching closer and closer to him.

When I saw my moment, I swiftly grabbed him and shut the door, trapping him inside my house, at last! He struggled, trying to get free. But I just held him close to me, softly talking to him. Finally, he seemed to relax a bit, so I started stroking him very gently. Then I let him down to roam around and investigate his new surroundings. When he wasn't looking, I moved his food bowl inside, cause I wasn't letting him out again for a few days.

I did not give him a name at first. I had no intentions of keeping him. I only wanted to help the baby. I planned to find him a good home after he was domesticated. He was not a particularly pretty kitten. He was really kind of comical looking. His ears looked too big for his head and they had crazy, wild hairs sticking out of them. His nose was splashed with different hues of orange and pink, like war paint! Litter training him was easy enough. He was a smart little boy and he made himself quite at home.

It seemed like divine timing for this kitten to show up when he did. I was not working, due to complications from Graves' disease. Many days I felt awful; my arms and legs felt like great weight hanging off me. I stayed in bed or on the sofa a lot. But now I had a reason to get up and care for this baby. He gave me something to think about outside of myself. He really needed me. He made me smile and laugh and that was worth a million dollars to me then.

When I would sit down on the couch, he would stop whatever he was doing, take a flying leap and jump up into my lap. If I happened to be drinking a beverage at that time, too bad! It would spill and splash all over me and him. He was so fast and rambunctious, just like a little boy. He loved to kiss my neck. He loved kissing me so much that I would have to make him stop. After a few days it dawned on me, this kitten loved me. He loved me before I really loved him! Looking at him with that revelation, I named him Jesse. He was a keeper.

Jesse really was a very funny cat! He seemed to sense I needed him as much as he needed me. He seemed to revel in making me laugh. I think he got as much pleasure out of me laughing as I did. I bought him a several toys and fixed up a box for him. When I'd get up in the morning, he'd have his toys scattered all over the living room floor! I would pretend to get on him and put them all back in his box. He would hang with me and watch, playing the game. He would sit and watch television with me too. He'd see me staring at the screen and he would stare at it with me. Jesse slept with me every night. He had a habit of trying to make my head his pillow. This would have been okay with me, accept he would purr straight into my ear, driving me crazy. I even fixed my pillow so he could put his head on that and lay beside me. But he would lay his body on the pillow and his head on my head. I'd never felt so loved!

I had him neutered and caught up on all his shots. He was turning out to be a very spunky and handsome boy after all. His fur was long and bright orange, with a beautiful fluffy plume tail. In the winter, his coat fluffed out, his face fur thickened and puffed up so he looked like Mufasa, from the Lion King. I believe he felt the part too. I was letting him outside some and he seemed to have no fear. This attitude made me fear for him. We would be out in the front yard and a dog would walk by on the road. Jesse would come to attention and stare after the dog, as if he might go after him! Was he protecting my property? The dog hastily moved on with his tail down between his legs. I was flabbergasted, as I hurriedly grabbed that cat up and took him in the house. "You're supposed to climb a tree, Jesse, not go after dogs!"

I never knew quite what to expect from him, he was so full of his antics. One early evening, he was playing on the front porch when I came to get him in for the night. He was sitting on the railing and I tried to pick him up, telling him, "Time to come in," well he wasn't ready to go in. He grabs for the railing post with both front paws and claws, hanging on for dear life. He was not letting go either! I only had one hand to hold him and one hand to try and pry his paws from around the post. I tugged and tugged, he wasn't budging. I could not help but giggle as I kept trying to get his paws unfastened from that post! I even begged him, "Jesse, please come on in the house!" Finally he gave in so I got him loose and carted him inside.

He played a similar antic again one evening. He was on the front porch and I again tell him it's time to go in. I tried to prod him along, as he slowly walks towards the front door. Suddenly he just plops down outside the doorway, in the floor. He looked just like a child refusing to walk for the very same reason. I totally lost it and sat down on the porch floor with him, just laughing hysterically at this furry clown!

We had many adventures and fun in the woods together. I had never had such a personable, little fur guy to care for and keep me company.

Jesse did not stay with me but 3 short years. I lost him to heartworms; neither his veterinarian nor I had any clue he suffered with them. He was always robust and healthy looking. He died having a stroke on my front porch, in front of me. It was 1 week before Christmas. All I could feel was emptiness and heartbreak with the loss of him. I kept asking God why He let this happen. I had been at church helping organize the Christmas music. When I got back home he seemed fine. I let him out for a few minutes on the porch; when I checked on him, he was having a stroke. It felt like I lost my mind that night. I cried for a long time, missing him terribly. I wasn't sure I would ever recover from losing him. Of course I did, but I have not gotten another cat since Jesse. Maybe one day in the future, another fur baby will find his or her way to me. I know I'll be ready.

Lost and Found

Always searching for my "self",
keep your heart on some high shelf,
lonely wandering, place to place.
Empty searching, face to face.
Wasting sweet and precious time,
too long waiting in wrong lines.

Scared to tear off untrue masks,
saving Jesus for the last.
And then, He quenches, hunger, thirst.
His desire, to save me first.

In finding Him, I found me,
far happier than I dreamed I'd be.
Better would my youth have been
if I'd only found Him then.

Being Big

In the summer of 2011, I drove down to Buckroe Beach, Virginia. My companion was Alexis, my dear friend's 3 year old daughter.

Alexis's mother, Kelly and I were not, biological sisters. We were sisters of the soul, which makes Alexis my niece of the soul. So she addresses me as, "Aunt Charlotte."

The day was sunny, warm and glorious. Alexis sat very alert, in the back secured by her carseat. I peeped at her often in the rearview mirror, as we chatted along the way. She was a blonde haired, blue eyed cherub, and I adored her. I excitedly told her all about the cool playground that sits right by the main waterfront and beach. In the midst of telling her about the different swings and climbing apparatus, she blew me away with a question.

"Are you big?"

Flabbergasted and amused, I stalled for time.

"What?"

She slowly and clearly repeated her question.

"Are…you…big?"

Did she take me for something like a ten-year-old, driving her to the beach? Her question struck me as funny but profound as well.

"Yes, but I have a child-like heart. That's why I love to play with you."

"Oh."

She seemed satisfied with my response and shortly she was snoozing and slept nearly the rest of the way there.

At the beach the water was terrific, cresting into the

sand, in small steady waves. We stood in the shallow water and I would lift her up so she'd not get spooked.

She had a blast and loved the water lightly splashing on us. We dug in the sand and played on each item in the playground. It was a wonderful day and I vowed we would return next year and do it all again.

About a week later, I thought of her question several times. It still struck me funny and always made me laugh.

I decided I had answered her well and prayed I would always have a child-like heart.

Then my thinking went further.

It felt like God was asking me a question.

"Well, how big are you?"

While considering the answer, even more questions started storming my mind.

Alexis

"Do you put yourself first or last? Do you think of others needs before your own? In the heat and turmoil of the moment, how long does it take you to make yourself last? Are you big enough to not gossip when it's all around you? Do you not make that cutting remark that hurts one person deeply while everyone else chuckles with laughter?"

"If perchance, you're still coming up big, how often are you big? Is it every day? All day? Twice a week? For five minutes, here and there? Once a year?"

"So, are you big?"

Perhaps I'd better change my answer to, "I have to work on it....daily."

Where would we be without 3-year olds to set us straight?

I thank you, Alexis!

Ocean Devotion

The young man stood at the ocean edge, looking out at the sea. He watched the waves build up and hurl towards him. Listening intently to the roar of the water, he closed his eyes and smiling to himself, breathed in the ocean air. He loved the sea. Often, he would go out in a small rowboat, to get away from the crowds, to think and to pray. As he walked along the shore, he knew he didn't have much time to do a quick work for his father. He realized he'd only have two or three years, at the most. But that's why he was here; to find a few good men and teach them to, "Love One Another." He had to show them how to build his church. But how could he teach them all they needed to learn, in such a short time? There was so much they needed to know. He thought about when he would need them the most, how they would fail him. Yet he would still cherish and adore each one. Because his Father and he were as one, the love was stronger, deeper, wider and higher than mankind could ever fathom it to be.

"Now as he walked beside the Sea of Galilee, he saw Simon and Andrew, his brother casting a net into the sea; for they were fishers. Jesus said to them, come ye after me, and I will make you fishers of men. Straightway they forsook their nets and followed him."

Mark 1: 16 – 18
Kill Devil Hills, North Carolina
April 26, 2002

Ocean

One night,
I watched as the ocean tide came in,
row upon row
of small waves
following the other.

I noticed,
the lines of waves broke up
into separate, smaller lines.

As the waves
broke into separate, swirling lines of foam,
each line extended itself,
stretching out to the breaking wave
of foam beside it.

Connecting with each other again,
they came rushing in, to the shore.

Closing Remarks

The one thing I have learned since my early years, Jesus has *been there and done that*. He was abandoned, abused, forsaken and forgotten. He became penniless to accomplish His mission. He did not have a *Clyde to ride*, much less a train or plane to get to any of the places He ministered. But He got there anyway and on time. He did not preach in a glorious church building and wore no plush robe or sparkling headdress. He was murdered by the officials and government of His day, for bogus crimes, He never committed. He suffered the slow, agonizing and painful death of crucifixion. He "KNOWS" how we feel; He has experienced it ALL for Himself.

In losing my biological parents, I used denial as my shelter. It shielded me from feeling the pain of abandonment and grief. At the time, that seemed to work. Denial is a lie, posing as a truth to set you free. It promises to be faster, easier and most important, less painful. Since then, I have found it better to embrace all that is within me, anger, pain and sorrow, handing all over to Jesus to fix. And He does just that. Then, He gives it back to you, as a testimony of Him. This gives Him the glory that He deserves. He wants to fix our brokenness, that's what He's for, as our Savior, our best friend. So many conflicts we have, come down to respect and loving one another, just like Jesus said. God has so wonderfully given us everything we need, each other, the animals and all the beautiful life forms. It seems to take our whole lifetime until we are *Big*. But He knew that all along, didn't He? What a great Dad and Shelter, He Is!

About the Author

CHARLOTTE ANN is an old- fashioned 69 year old country girl. She was born and raised in Richmond, Virginia, in 1950. Her parents were very young and ill equipped to raise an infant. She was placed in a foster home as a new-born baby. Her foster mother kept infants for the welfare department; Charlotte grew up caring for infants, as well. She, like her foster siblings, bottle fed, changed diapers, and cared for many homeless children, like herself.

Later in life, she was drawn to work for the Richmond SPCA. There she discovered her love for animals and also that she had a talent for writing.

She left the shelter, to expand her knowledge in the health and medical field, increasing her skills as an employee.

Never forgetting about the animals, she wrote about them, through the years, correlating them together with her own background of abandonment and loss. Her style of writing falls somewhere between Hellen Steiner Rice and Shel Silverstein. Today Charlotte lives in rural Virginia with her son, Jon.

Printed in the United States
By Bookmasters